I0006408

About My Blog

Purpose Of My Blog	Why does your blog exist?
Target Audience	Who do want to attract?
What I Offer	What do you offer your readers?
How I Promote	How do you promote your blog?
Money	Do you monetize your blog? How?

My Blog Categories

Category #1

Sub-Categories
- ○
- ○
- ○

Category #2

Sub-Categories
- ○
- ○
- ○

Category #3

Sub-Categories
- ○
- ○
- ○

Category #4

Sub-Categories
- ○
- ○
- ○

Category #5

Sub-Categories
- ○
- ○
- ○

Category #6

Sub-Categories
- ○
- ○
- ○

Blog Tags I Use

Tag	In Category	For Topic

Blog Post Index

✓	Post Title	Category	Pages

✓	Post Title	Category	Pages

◯ Blog title:	

Publish date:	Category:

Quick Post Summary	What exactly are you aiming for?

Main Keywords	SEO	Pinterest
	◯	◯
	◯	◯
	◯	◯
	◯	◯
	◯	◯

Opt-in Offer	Are you offering a freebie/upgrade?

Heading #1	
Heading #2	
Heading #3	
Heading #4	
Heading #5	

Research Points

What research is needed for this?

- ○
- ○
- ○
- ○

Affiliate Products

Are you promoting any products?

- ○
- ○
- ○
- ○

Social Media Plan

What's the social media plan for this?

Blog Post Checklist

○ Catchy title	○ Descriptions written
○ Keyworded	○ Affiliate links added
○ Images made	○ Internal links
○ Headings	○ Call to action
○ Checked & edited	○ Social media scheduled
○	○
○	○

Blog title:

Publish date: **Category:**

Quick Post Summary

What exactly are you aiming for?

Main Keywords

SEO	Pinterest
○	○
○	○
○	○
○	○
○	○

Opt-in Offer

Are you offering a freebie/upgrade?

Heading #1

Heading #2

Heading #3

Heading #4

Heading #5

Research Points

What research is needed for this?

- ○
- ○
- ○
- ○

Affiliate Products

Are you promoting any products?

- ○
- ○
- ○
- ○

Social Media Plan

What's the social media plan for this?

Blog Post Checklist

○ Catchy title	○ Descriptions written
○ Keyworded	○ Affiliate links added
○ Images made	○ Internal links
○ Headings	○ Call to action
○ Checked & edited	○ Social media scheduled
○	○
○	○

◯ Blog title:	

Publish date:	Category:

Quick Post Summary	What exactly are you aiming for?

Main Keywords	SEO	Pinterest
	◯	◯
	◯	◯
	◯	◯
	◯	◯
	◯	◯

Opt-in Offer	Are you offering a freebie/upgrade?

Heading #1	
Heading #2	
Heading #3	
Heading #4	
Heading #5	

Research Points

What research is needed for this? ○

- ○
- ○
- ○
- ○

Affiliate Products

Are you promoting any products?

- ○
- ○
- ○
- ○

Social Media Plan

What's the social media plan for this?

Blog Post Checklist

○	Catchy title	○	Descriptions written
○	Keyworded	○	Affiliate links added
○	Images made	○	Internal links
○	Headings	○	Call to action
○	Checked & edited	○	Social media scheduled
○		○	
○		○	

⊙ Blog title:	

Publish date:	Category:

Quick Post Summary	What exactly are you aiming for?

Main Keywords	SEO	Pinterest
	○	○
	○	○
	○	○
	○	○
	○	○

Opt-in Offer	Are you offering a freebie/upgrade?

Heading #1	
Heading #2	
Heading #3	
Heading #4	
Heading #5	

Research Points

What research is needed for this?

- O
- O
- O
- O

Affiliate Products

Are you promoting any products?

- O
- O
- O
- O

Social Media Plan

What's the social media plan for this?

Blog Post Checklist

O	Catchy title	O	Descriptions written
O	Keyworded	O	Affiliate links added
O	Images made	O	Internal links
O	Headings	O	Call to action
O	Checked & edited	O	Social media scheduled
O		O	
O		O	

⭕ Blog title:	

Publish date:	Category:

Quick Post Summary	What exactly are you aiming for?

Main Keywords	SEO ○ ○ ○ ○ ○	Pinterest ○ ○ ○ ○ ○

Opt-in Offer	Are you offering a freebie/upgrade?

Heading #1	
Heading #2	
Heading #3	
Heading #4	
Heading #5	

Research Points

What research is needed for this?

-
-
-
-

Affiliate Products

Are you promoting any products?

-
-
-
-

Social Media Plan

What's the social media plan for this?

Blog Post Checklist	
○ Catchy title	○ Descriptions written
○ Keyworded	○ Affiliate links added
○ Images made	○ Internal links
○ Headings	○ Call to action
○ Checked & edited	○ Social media scheduled
○	○
○	○

◯ Blog title:	

Publish date:	Category:

Quick Post Summary	What exactly are you aiming for?

Main Keywords	SEO	Pinterest
	◯	◯
	◯	◯
	◯	◯
	◯	◯
	◯	◯

Opt-in Offer	Are you offering a freebie/upgrade?

Heading #1	
Heading #2	
Heading #3	
Heading #4	
Heading #5	

Research Points

What research is needed for this?

- ○
- ○
- ○
- ○

Affiliate Products

Are you promoting any products?

- ○
- ○
- ○
- ○

Social Media Plan

What's the social media plan for this?

Blog Post Checklist

○	Catchy title	○	Descriptions written
○	Keyworded	○	Affiliate links added
○	Images made	○	Internal links
○	Headings	○	Call to action
○	Checked & edited	○	Social media scheduled
○		○	
○		○	

| Blog title: | |

Publish date: **Category:**

| Quick Post Summary | What exactly are you aiming for? |

Main Keywords	SEO	Pinterest
	○	○
	○	○
	○	○
	○	○
	○	○

| Opt-in Offer | Are you offering a freebie/upgrade? |

Heading #1	
Heading #2	
Heading #3	
Heading #4	
Heading #5	

Research Points	What research is needed for this? ⭕
	○
	○
	○
	○

Affiliate Products	Are you promoting any products?
	○
	○
	○
	○

Social Media Plan	What's the social media plan for this?

Blog Post Checklist

○ Catchy title		○ Descriptions written
○ Keyworded		○ Affiliate links added
○ Images made		○ Internal links
○ Headings		○ Call to action
○ Checked & edited		○ Social media scheduled
○		○
○		○

Blog title:	

Publish date:	Category:

Quick Post Summary	What exactly are you aiming for?

Main Keywords	SEO	Pinterest
	○	○
	○	○
	○	○
	○	○
	○	○

Opt-in Offer	Are you offering a freebie/upgrade?

Heading #1	
Heading #2	
Heading #3	
Heading #4	
Heading #5	

Research Points

What research is needed for this?

- ○
- ○
- ○
- ○

Affiliate Products

Are you promoting any products?

- ○
- ○
- ○
- ○

Social Media Plan

What's the social media plan for this?

Blog Post Checklist

○	Catchy title	○	Descriptions written
○	Keyworded	○	Affiliate links added
○	Images made	○	Internal links
○	Headings	○	Call to action
○	Checked & edited	○	Social media scheduled
○		○	
○		○	

Blog title:	

Publish date:	Category:

Quick Post Summary	What exactly are you aiming for?

Main Keywords	SEO	Pinterest
	○	○
	○	○
	○	○
	○	○
	○	○

Opt-in Offer	Are you offering a freebie/upgrade?

Heading #1	
Heading #2	
Heading #3	
Heading #4	
Heading #5	

Research Points

What research is needed for this?

- ○
- ○
- ○
- ○

Affiliate Products

Are you promoting any products?

- ○
- ○
- ○
- ○

Social Media Plan

What's the social media plan for this?

Blog Post Checklist

○ Catchy title	○ Descriptions written
○ Keyworded	○ Affiliate links added
○ Images made	○ Internal links
○ Headings	○ Call to action
○ Checked & edited	○ Social media scheduled
○	○
○	○

Blog title:

Publish date: **Category:**

Quick Post Summary

What exactly are you aiming for?

Main Keywords

SEO	Pinterest
○	○
○	○
○	○
○	○
○	○

Opt-in Offer

Are you offering a freebie/upgrade?

Heading #1

Heading #2

Heading #3

Heading #4

Heading #5

Research Points

What research is needed for this?

- ○
- ○
- ○
- ○

Affiliate Products

Are you promoting any products?

- ○
- ○
- ○
- ○

Social Media Plan

What's the social media plan for this?

Blog Post Checklist

○ Catchy title	○ Descriptions written
○ Keyworded	○ Affiliate links added
○ Images made	○ Internal links
○ Headings	○ Call to action
○ Checked & edited	○ Social media scheduled
○	○
○	○

Blog title:

Publish date: | **Category:**

Quick Post Summary

What exactly are you aiming for?

Main Keywords

SEO	Pinterest
○	○
○	○
○	○
○	○
○	○

Opt-in Offer

Are you offering a freebie/upgrade?

Heading #1

Heading #2

Heading #3

Heading #4

Heading #5

Research Points

What research is needed for this?

- ○
- ○
- ○
- ○

Affiliate Products

Are you promoting any products?

- ○
- ○
- ○
- ○

Social Media Plan

What's the social media plan for this?

Blog Post Checklist

○	Catchy title	○	Descriptions written
○	Keyworded	○	Affiliate links added
○	Images made	○	Internal links
○	Headings	○	Call to action
○	Checked & edited	○	Social media scheduled
○		○	
○		○	

Blog title:	

Publish date:	Category:

Quick Post Summary	What exactly are you aiming for?

	SEO	Pinterest
Main Keywords	○ ○ ○ ○ ○	○ ○ ○ ○ ○

Opt-in Offer	Are you offering a freebie/upgrade?

Heading #1	
Heading #2	
Heading #3	
Heading #4	
Heading #5	

Research Points

What research is needed for this?

- ○
- ○
- ○
- ○

Affiliate Products

Are you promoting any products?

- ○
- ○
- ○
- ○

Social Media Plan

What's the social media plan for this?

Blog Post Checklist

○ Catchy title	○ Descriptions written
○ Keyworded	○ Affiliate links added
○ Images made	○ Internal links
○ Headings	○ Call to action
○ Checked & edited	○ Social media scheduled
○	○
○	○

Blog title:

Publish date: | **Category:**

Quick Post Summary | What exactly are you aiming for?

Main Keywords

SEO	Pinterest
○	○
○	○
○	○
○	○
○	○

Opt-in Offer | Are you offering a freebie/upgrade?

Heading #1

Heading #2

Heading #3

Heading #4

Heading #5

Research Points

What research is needed for this?

- ○
- ○
- ○
- ○

Affiliate Products

Are you promoting any products?

- ○
- ○
- ○
- ○

Social Media Plan

What's the social media plan for this?

Blog Post Checklist

○ Catchy title	○ Descriptions written
○ Keyworded	○ Affiliate links added
○ Images made	○ Internal links
○ Headings	○ Call to action
○ Checked & edited	○ Social media scheduled
○	○
○	○

Blog title:

Publish date: | **Category:**

Quick Post Summary | What exactly are you aiming for?

Main Keywords

	SEO		Pinterest
○		○	
○		○	
○		○	
○		○	
○		○	

Opt-in Offer | Are you offering a freebie/upgrade?

Heading #1 |

Heading #2 |

Heading #3 |

Heading #4 |

Heading #5 |

Research Points

What research is needed for this?

- ○
- ○
- ○
- ○

Affiliate Products

Are you promoting any products?

- ○
- ○
- ○
- ○

Social Media Plan

What's the social media plan for this?

Blog Post Checklist	
○ Catchy title	○ Descriptions written
○ Keyworded	○ Affiliate links added
○ Images made	○ Internal links
○ Headings	○ Call to action
○ Checked & edited	○ Social media scheduled
○	○
○	○

◯ Blog title:	

Publish date:	Category:

Quick Post Summary	What exactly are you aiming for?

	SEO	Pinterest
Main Keywords	◯ ◯ ◯ ◯ ◯	◯ ◯ ◯ ◯ ◯

Opt-in Offer	Are you offering a freebie/upgrade?

Heading #1	
Heading #2	
Heading #3	
Heading #4	
Heading #5	

Research Points

What research is needed for this?

- ○
- ○
- ○
- ○

Affiliate Products

Are you promoting any products?

- ○
- ○
- ○
- ○

Social Media Plan

What's the social media plan for this?

Blog Post Checklist

○ Catchy title	○ Descriptions written
○ Keyworded	○ Affiliate links added
○ Images made	○ Internal links
○ Headings	○ Call to action
○ Checked & edited	○ Social media scheduled
○	○
○	○

Blog title:

Publish date: **Category:**

Quick Post Summary — What exactly are you aiming for?

Main Keywords

SEO	Pinterest
○	○
○	○
○	○
○	○
○	○

Opt-in Offer — Are you offering a freebie/upgrade?

Heading #1

Heading #2

Heading #3

Heading #4

Heading #5

Research Points

What research is needed for this?

- ○
- ○
- ○
- ○

Affiliate Products

Are you promoting any products?

- ○
- ○
- ○
- ○

Social Media Plan

What's the social media plan for this?

Blog Post Checklist

○	Catchy title	○	Descriptions written
○	Keyworded	○	Affiliate links added
○	Images made	○	Internal links
○	Headings	○	Call to action
○	Checked & edited	○	Social media scheduled
○		○	
○		○	

Blog title:	

Publish date:	Category:

Quick Post Summary	What exactly are you aiming for?

	SEO	Pinterest
Main Keywords	○ ○ ○ ○ ○	○ ○ ○ ○ ○

Opt-in Offer	Are you offering a freebie/upgrade?

Heading #1	
Heading #2	
Heading #3	
Heading #4	
Heading #5	

Research Points

What research is needed for this?

- ○
- ○
- ○
- ○

Affiliate Products

Are you promoting any products?

- ○
- ○
- ○
- ○

Social Media Plan

What's the social media plan for this?

Blog Post Checklist

○	Catchy title	○	Descriptions written
○	Keyworded	○	Affiliate links added
○	Images made	○	Internal links
○	Headings	○	Call to action
○	Checked & edited	○	Social media scheduled
○		○	
○		○	

◯ Blog title:	

Publish date:	Category:

Quick Post Summary	What exactly are you aiming for?

Main Keywords	SEO	Pinterest
	◯	◯
	◯	◯
	◯	◯
	◯	◯
	◯	◯

Opt-in Offer	Are you offering a freebie/upgrade?

Heading #1	
Heading #2	
Heading #3	
Heading #4	
Heading #5	

Research Points

What research is needed for this?

- ○
- ○
- ○
- ○

Affiliate Products

Are you promoting any products?

- ○
- ○
- ○
- ○

Social Media Plan

What's the social media plan for this?

Blog Post Checklist

○	Catchy title	○	Descriptions written
○	Keyworded	○	Affiliate links added
○	Images made	○	Internal links
○	Headings	○	Call to action
○	Checked & edited	○	Social media scheduled
○		○	
○		○	

Blog title:

Publish date: **Category:**

Quick Post Summary

What exactly are you aiming for?

Main Keywords

SEO Pinterest

○ ○
○ ○
○ ○
○ ○
○ ○

Opt-in Offer

Are you offering a freebie/upgrade?

Heading #1

Heading #2

Heading #3

Heading #4

Heading #5

Research Points

What research is needed for this?

- o
- o
- o
- o

Affiliate Products

Are you promoting any products?

- o
- o
- o
- o

Social Media Plan

What's the social media plan for this?

Blog Post Checklist

o	Catchy title	o	Descriptions written
o	Keyworded	o	Affiliate links added
o	Images made	o	Internal links
o	Headings	o	Call to action
o	Checked & edited	o	Social media scheduled
o		o	
o		o	

○ Blog title:

Publish date: | Category:

Quick Post Summary

What exactly are you aiming for?

Main Keywords

SEO | Pinterest
○ | ○
○ | ○
○ | ○
○ | ○
○ | ○

Opt-in Offer

Are you offering a freebie/upgrade?

Heading #1

Heading #2

Heading #3

Heading #4

Heading #5

Research Points

What research is needed for this?

- ○
- ○
- ○
- ○

Affiliate Products

Are you promoting any products?

- ○
- ○
- ○
- ○

Social Media Plan

What's the social media plan for this?

Blog Post Checklist

○	Catchy title	○	Descriptions written
○	Keyworded	○	Affiliate links added
○	Images made	○	Internal links
○	Headings	○	Call to action
○	Checked & edited	○	Social media scheduled
○		○	
○		○	

Blog title:

Publish date: **Category:**

Quick Post Summary — What exactly are you aiming for?

Main Keywords

SEO	Pinterest
○	○
○	○
○	○
○	○
○	○

Opt-in Offer — Are you offering a freebie/upgrade?

Heading #1

Heading #2

Heading #3

Heading #4

Heading #5

Research Points

What research is needed for this?

- ○
- ○
- ○
- ○

Affiliate Products

Are you promoting any products?

- ○
- ○
- ○
- ○

Social Media Plan

What's the social media plan for this?

Blog Post Checklist

○ Catchy title	○ Descriptions written
○ Keyworded	○ Affiliate links added
○ Images made	○ Internal links
○ Headings	○ Call to action
○ Checked & edited	○ Social media scheduled
○	○
○	○

	Blog title:

Publish date:	Category:

Quick Post Summary	What exactly are you aiming for?

Main Keywords	SEO	Pinterest
	○	○
	○	○
	○	○
	○	○
	○	○

Opt-in Offer	Are you offering a freebie/upgrade?

Heading #1	
Heading #2	
Heading #3	
Heading #4	
Heading #5	

Research Points

What research is needed for this?

- ○
- ○
- ○
- ○

Affiliate Products

Are you promoting any products?

- ○
- ○
- ○
- ○

Social Media Plan

What's the social media plan for this?

Blog Post Checklist

○ Catchy title	○ Descriptions written
○ Keyworded	○ Affiliate links added
○ Images made	○ Internal links
○ Headings	○ Call to action
○ Checked & edited	○ Social media scheduled
○	○
○	○

Blog title:

Publish date: **Category:**

Quick Post Summary

What exactly are you aiming for?

Main Keywords

SEO	Pinterest
○	○
○	○
○	○
○	○
○	○

Opt-in Offer

Are you offering a freebie/upgrade?

Heading #1

Heading #2

Heading #3

Heading #4

Heading #5

Research Points

What research is needed for this?

- ○
- ○
- ○
- ○

Affiliate Products

Are you promoting any products?

- ○
- ○
- ○
- ○

Social Media Plan

What's the social media plan for this?

Blog Post Checklist

○	Catchy title	○	Descriptions written
○	Keyworded	○	Affiliate links added
○	Images made	○	Internal links
○	Headings	○	Call to action
○	Checked & edited	○	Social media scheduled
○		○	
○		○	

Blog title:	

Publish date:	Category:

Quick Post Summary	What exactly are you aiming for?

Main Keywords

	SEO	Pinterest
	○	○
	○	○
	○	○
	○	○
	○	○

Opt-in Offer	Are you offering a freebie/upgrade?

Heading #1	
Heading #2	
Heading #3	
Heading #4	
Heading #5	

Research Points

What research is needed for this?

- ○
- ○
- ○
- ○

Affiliate Products

Are you promoting any products?

- ○
- ○
- ○
- ○

Social Media Plan

What's the social media plan for this?

Blog Post Checklist

○ Catchy title	○ Descriptions written
○ Keyworded	○ Affiliate links added
○ Images made	○ Internal links
○ Headings	○ Call to action
○ Checked & edited	○ Social media scheduled
○	○
○	○

Blog title:

Publish date: **Category:**

Quick Post Summary

What exactly are you aiming for?

Main Keywords

SEO	Pinterest
○	○
○	○
○	○
○	○
○	○

Opt-in Offer

Are you offering a freebie/upgrade?

Heading #1

Heading #2

Heading #3

Heading #4

Heading #5

Research Points

What research is needed for this?

- ○
- ○
- ○
- ○

Affiliate Products

Are you promoting any products?

- ○
- ○
- ○
- ○

Social Media Plan

What's the social media plan for this?

Blog Post Checklist

○ Catchy title	○ Descriptions written
○ Keyworded	○ Affiliate links added
○ Images made	○ Internal links
○ Headings	○ Call to action
○ Checked & edited	○ Social media scheduled
○	○
○	○

Blog title:	

Publish date:	Category:

Quick Post Summary	What exactly are you aiming for?

Main Keywords	SEO	Pinterest
	○	○
	○	○
	○	○
	○	○
	○	○

Opt-in Offer	Are you offering a freebie/upgrade?

Heading #1	
Heading #2	
Heading #3	
Heading #4	
Heading #5	

Research Points

What research is needed for this?

- ○
- ○
- ○
- ○

Affiliate Products

Are you promoting any products?

- ○
- ○
- ○
- ○

Social Media Plan

What's the social media plan for this?

Blog Post Checklist

○ Catchy title	○ Descriptions written
○ Keyworded	○ Affiliate links added
○ Images made	○ Internal links
○ Headings	○ Call to action
○ Checked & edited	○ Social media scheduled
○	○
○	○

Blog title:	

Publish date:	Category:

Quick Post Summary	What exactly are you aiming for?

Main Keywords	SEO	Pinterest
	○	○
	○	○
	○	○
	○	○
	○	○

Opt-in Offer	Are you offering a freebie/upgrade?

Heading #1	
Heading #2	
Heading #3	
Heading #4	
Heading #5	

Research Points

What research is needed for this?

- ○
- ○
- ○
- ○

Affiliate Products

Are you promoting any products?

- ○
- ○
- ○
- ○

Social Media Plan

What's the social media plan for this?

Blog Post Checklist

○	Catchy title	○	Descriptions written
○	Keyworded	○	Affiliate links added
○	Images made	○	Internal links
○	Headings	○	Call to action
○	Checked & edited	○	Social media scheduled
○		○	
○		○	

Blog title:

Publish date: **Category:**

Quick Post Summary

What exactly are you aiming for?

Main Keywords

SEO	Pinterest
○	○
○	○
○	○
○	○
○	○

Opt-in Offer

Are you offering a freebie/upgrade?

Heading #1	
Heading #2	
Heading #3	
Heading #4	
Heading #5	

Research Points

What research is needed for this?

- ○
- ○
- ○
- ○

Affiliate Products

Are you promoting any products?

- ○
- ○
- ○
- ○

Social Media Plan

What's the social media plan for this?

Blog Post Checklist

○ Catchy title	○ Descriptions written
○ Keyworded	○ Affiliate links added
○ Images made	○ Internal links
○ Headings	○ Call to action
○ Checked & edited	○ Social media scheduled
○	○
○	○

Blog title:

Publish date: **Category:**

Quick Post Summary

What exactly are you aiming for?

Main Keywords

SEO	Pinterest
○	○
○	○
○	○
○	○
○	○

Opt-in Offer

Are you offering a freebie/upgrade?

Heading #1

Heading #2

Heading #3

Heading #4

Heading #5

Research Points

What research is needed for this?

- ○
- ○
- ○
- ○

Affiliate Products

Are you promoting any products?

- ○
- ○
- ○
- ○

Social Media Plan

What's the social media plan for this?

Blog Post Checklist

○ Catchy title	○ Descriptions written
○ Keyworded	○ Affiliate links added
○ Images made	○ Internal links
○ Headings	○ Call to action
○ Checked & edited	○ Social media scheduled
○	○
○	○

Blog title:

Publish date: **Category:**

Quick Post Summary

What exactly are you aiming for?

Main Keywords

SEO	Pinterest
○	○
○	○
○	○
○	○
○	○

Opt-in Offer

Are you offering a freebie/upgrade?

Heading #1

Heading #2

Heading #3

Heading #4

Heading #5

Research Points

What research is needed for this?

- ○
- ○
- ○
- ○

Affiliate Products

Are you promoting any products?

- ○
- ○
- ○
- ○

Social Media Plan

What's the social media plan for this?

Blog Post Checklist

○	Catchy title	○	Descriptions written
○	Keyworded	○	Affiliate links added
○	Images made	○	Internal links
○	Headings	○	Call to action
○	Checked & edited	○	Social media scheduled
○		○	
○		○	

○ Blog title:	

Publish date:	Category:

Quick Post Summary	What exactly are you aiming for?

Main Keywords	SEO	Pinterest
	○	○
	○	○
	○	○
	○	○
	○	○

Opt-in Offer	Are you offering a freebie/upgrade?

Heading #1	
Heading #2	
Heading #3	
Heading #4	
Heading #5	

Research Points

What research is needed for this?

- ○
- ○
- ○
- ○

Affiliate Products

Are you promoting any products?

- ○
- ○
- ○
- ○

Social Media Plan

What's the social media plan for this?

Blog Post Checklist

○	Catchy title	○	Descriptions written
○	Keyworded	○	Affiliate links added
○	Images made	○	Internal links
○	Headings	○	Call to action
○	Checked & edited	○	Social media scheduled
○		○	
○		○	

Blog title:

Publish date: **Category:**

Quick Post Summary

What exactly are you aiming for?

Main Keywords

SEO	Pinterest
○	○
○	○
○	○
○	○
○	○

Opt-in Offer

Are you offering a freebie/upgrade?

Heading #1

Heading #2

Heading #3

Heading #4

Heading #5

Research Points

What research is needed for this?

- ○
- ○
- ○
- ○

Affiliate Products

Are you promoting any products?

- ○
- ○
- ○
- ○

Social Media Plan

What's the social media plan for this?

Blog Post Checklist

○ Catchy title	○ Descriptions written
○ Keyworded	○ Affiliate links added
○ Images made	○ Internal links
○ Headings	○ Call to action
○ Checked & edited	○ Social media scheduled
○	○
○	○

Blog title:

Publish date: **Category:**

Quick Post Summary

What exactly are you aiming for?

Main Keywords

SEO	Pinterest
○	○
○	○
○	○
○	○
○	○

Opt-in Offer

Are you offering a freebie/upgrade?

Heading #1

Heading #2

Heading #3

Heading #4

Heading #5

Research Points	What research is needed for this? ⭕
	○
	○
	○
	○

Affiliate Products	Are you promoting any products?
	○
	○
	○
	○

Social Media Plan	What's the social media plan for this?

Blog Post Checklist

○	Catchy title	○	Descriptions written
○	Keyworded	○	Affiliate links added
○	Images made	○	Internal links
○	Headings	○	Call to action
○	Checked & edited	○	Social media scheduled
○		○	
○		○	

◯ **Blog title:**	

Publish date:	**Category:**

Quick Post Summary	**What exactly are you aiming for?**

	SEO	Pinterest
Main Keywords	◯ ◯ ◯ ◯ ◯	◯ ◯ ◯ ◯ ◯

Opt-in Offer	**Are you offering a freebie/upgrade?**

Heading #1	
Heading #2	
Heading #3	
Heading #4	
Heading #5	

Research Points

What research is needed for this?

- ○
- ○
- ○
- ○

Affiliate Products

Are you promoting any products?

- ○
- ○
- ○
- ○

Social Media Plan

What's the social media plan for this?

Blog Post Checklist

○ Catchy title	○ Descriptions written
○ Keyworded	○ Affiliate links added
○ Images made	○ Internal links
○ Headings	○ Call to action
○ Checked & edited	○ Social media scheduled
○	○
○	○

◯ Blog title:	

Publish date:	Category:

Quick Post Summary	What exactly are you aiming for?

Main Keywords	SEO	Pinterest
	◯	◯
	◯	◯
	◯	◯
	◯	◯
	◯	◯

Opt-in Offer	Are you offering a freebie/upgrade?

Heading #1	
Heading #2	
Heading #3	
Heading #4	
Heading #5	

Research Points

What research is needed for this?

- ○
- ○
- ○
- ○

Affiliate Products

Are you promoting any products?

- ○
- ○
- ○
- ○

Social Media Plan

What's the social media plan for this?

Blog Post Checklist

○ Catchy title	○ Descriptions written
○ Keyworded	○ Affiliate links added
○ Images made	○ Internal links
○ Headings	○ Call to action
○ Checked & edited	○ Social media scheduled
○	○
○	○

○ Blog title:	

Publish date:	Category:

Quick Post Summary	What exactly are you aiming for?

Main Keywords	SEO	Pinterest
	○	○
	○	○
	○	○
	○	○
	○	○

Opt-in Offer	Are you offering a freebie/upgrade?

Heading #1	
Heading #2	
Heading #3	
Heading #4	
Heading #5	

Research Points

What research is needed for this?

- ○
- ○
- ○
- ○

Affiliate Products

Are you promoting any products?

- ○
- ○
- ○
- ○

Social Media Plan

What's the social media plan for this?

Blog Post Checklist

○ Catchy title	○ Descriptions written
○ Keyworded	○ Affiliate links added
○ Images made	○ Internal links
○ Headings	○ Call to action
○ Checked & edited	○ Social media scheduled
○	○
○	○

	Blog title:	

Publish date:	Category:

Quick Post Summary	What exactly are you aiming for?

Main Keywords	SEO	Pinterest
	○	○
	○	○
	○	○
	○	○
	○	○

Opt-in Offer	Are you offering a freebie/upgrade?

Heading #1	
Heading #2	
Heading #3	
Heading #4	
Heading #5	

Research Points

What research is needed for this?

- ○
- ○
- ○
- ○

Affiliate Products

Are you promoting any products?

- ○
- ○
- ○
- ○

Social Media Plan

What's the social media plan for this?

Blog Post Checklist

○ Catchy title	○ Descriptions written
○ Keyworded	○ Affiliate links added
○ Images made	○ Internal links
○ Headings	○ Call to action
○ Checked & edited	○ Social media scheduled
○	○
○	○

○ Blog title:	

Publish date:	Category:

Quick Post Summary	What exactly are you aiming for?

Main Keywords	SEO	Pinterest
	○	○
	○	○
	○	○
	○	○
	○	○

Opt-in Offer	Are you offering a freebie/upgrade?

Heading #1	
Heading #2	
Heading #3	
Heading #4	
Heading #5	

Research Points

What research is needed for this?

- ○
- ○
- ○
- ○

Affiliate Products

Are you promoting any products?

- ○
- ○
- ○
- ○

Social Media Plan

What's the social media plan for this?

Blog Post Checklist

○ Catchy title	○ Descriptions written
○ Keyworded	○ Affiliate links added
○ Images made	○ Internal links
○ Headings	○ Call to action
○ Checked & edited	○ Social media scheduled
○	○
○	○

Blog title:

Publish date: **Category:**

Quick Post Summary

What exactly are you aiming for?

Main Keywords

	SEO	Pinterest
	○	○
	○	○
	○	○
	○	○
	○	○

Opt-in Offer

Are you offering a freebie/upgrade?

Heading #1

Heading #2

Heading #3

Heading #4

Heading #5

Research Points

What research is needed for this?

- ○
- ○
- ○
- ○

Affiliate Products

Are you promoting any products?

- ○
- ○
- ○
- ○

Social Media Plan

What's the social media plan for this?

Blog Post Checklist

○ Catchy title	○ Descriptions written
○ Keyworded	○ Affiliate links added
○ Images made	○ Internal links
○ Headings	○ Call to action
○ Checked & edited	○ Social media scheduled
○	○
○	○

Blog title:

Publish date: **Category:**

Quick Post Summary

What exactly are you aiming for?

Main Keywords

SEO	Pinterest
O	O
O	O
O	O
O	O
O	O

Opt-in Offer

Are you offering a freebie/upgrade?

Heading #1

Heading #2

Heading #3

Heading #4

Heading #5

Research Points

What research is needed for this?

- ○
- ○
- ○
- ○

Affiliate Products

Are you promoting any products?

- ○
- ○
- ○
- ○

Social Media Plan

What's the social media plan for this?

Blog Post Checklist	
○ Catchy title	○ Descriptions written
○ Keyworded	○ Affiliate links added
○ Images made	○ Internal links
○ Headings	○ Call to action
○ Checked & edited	○ Social media scheduled
○	○
○	○

Blog title:

Publish date: | **Category:**

Quick Post Summary | What exactly are you aiming for?

Main Keywords

	SEO		Pinterest
○		○	
○		○	
○		○	
○		○	
○		○	

Opt-in Offer | Are you offering a freebie/upgrade?

Heading #1

Heading #2

Heading #3

Heading #4

Heading #5

Research Points

What research is needed for this?

- ○
- ○
- ○
- ○

Affiliate Products

Are you promoting any products?

- ○
- ○
- ○
- ○

Social Media Plan

What's the social media plan for this?

Blog Post Checklist

○ Catchy title	○ Descriptions written
○ Keyworded	○ Affiliate links added
○ Images made	○ Internal links
○ Headings	○ Call to action
○ Checked & edited	○ Social media scheduled
○	○
○	○

⬤ Blog title:	

Publish date:	Category:

Quick Post Summary	What exactly are you aiming for?

Main Keywords	**SEO** ○ ○ ○ ○ ○	**Pinterest** ○ ○ ○ ○ ○

Opt-in Offer	Are you offering a freebie/upgrade?

Heading #1	
Heading #2	
Heading #3	
Heading #4	
Heading #5	

Research Points

What research is needed for this?

- ○
- ○
- ○
- ○

Affiliate Products

Are you promoting any products?

- ○
- ○
- ○
- ○

Social Media Plan

What's the social media plan for this?

Blog Post Checklist	
○ Catchy title	○ Descriptions written
○ Keyworded	○ Affiliate links added
○ Images made	○ Internal links
○ Headings	○ Call to action
○ Checked & edited	○ Social media scheduled
○	○
○	○

◯ Blog title:	

Publish date:	Category:

Quick Post Summary	What exactly are you aiming for?

Main Keywords	SEO	Pinterest
	◯	◯
	◯	◯
	◯	◯
	◯	◯
	◯	◯

Opt-in Offer	Are you offering a freebie/upgrade?

Heading #1	
Heading #2	
Heading #3	
Heading #4	
Heading #5	

Research Points

What research is needed for this?

- ○
- ○
- ○
- ○

Affiliate Products

Are you promoting any products?

- ○
- ○
- ○
- ○

Social Media Plan

What's the social media plan for this?

Blog Post Checklist

○ Catchy title	○ Descriptions written
○ Keyworded	○ Affiliate links added
○ Images made	○ Internal links
○ Headings	○ Call to action
○ Checked & edited	○ Social media scheduled
○	○
○	○

www.ingramcontent.com/pod-product-compliance
Lightning Source LLC
Chambersburg PA
CBHW051209050326
40689CB00008B/1248

* 9 7 8 1 0 9 3 2 6 0 3 4 2 *